HOME GOING
POETRY FOR A SEASON

BY CAROLYN WEBER

ANO ZETEO PRESS

For queries on permissions, international rights or
discounted quantity ordering, please contact the publisher at
AnoZeteo.com

AnoZeteo

Copyright © 2015 by Carolyn Weber
Cover photo: © coyote

Library of Congress Cataloging-in-Publication Data:
application in process

ISBN (PprBk): 978-0-9880572-9-6
ISBN (eBook): 978-1-987897-00-5

First printed in the United States of America.
This first edition March 2015

2 4 6 8 10 9 7 5 3 1

For all those who long for home

Table of Contents

Preface

This collection combines three sets of poems. The first group are new, having been written over the course of this last year. The second groups, *True North* and *Summering*, were originally published under the same names respectively, but now gathered here under this single volume entitled inclusively *Home Going*. My title is purposely evocative of Philip Larkin's wonderful poem and pun "Church Going." What is this compulsion we have to revisit places, and particularly to go home? And yet, like churches, what purposes do these spaces serve, and what are their both temporal and timeless meanings in our spiritual pilgrimages?

I left Canada as a student of literature, and remained outside of Canada for many years as a teacher of literature. Now I return to Canada as a deliberate writer of words, having walked through the looking glass, so to speak, and entered what I used to think I understood so well. George Eliot had once remarked that when people said they had seen through a thing they usually meant they hadn't seen it at all. On the other side now, I find I cannot comprehend fully what I thought I knew so well. And that is a great gift. For any gift truly worth having – friendship, insight, joy, love, humility, wisdom – cannot be held in the hand. But poetry, as an act of gifting, I now see, has never come from closure or control.

In expressing the elusive beauty of the birds in the bush, we must lay down the one in our hand. And so we have no alternative but to turn to poetry – it is the only place of expression, of rest, that acknowledges the tension between how deeply we feel things and how utterly inexpressible those feelings are. Poetry offers the depths and the heights of human experience, where we bury and resurrect our dead. Poetry becomes where we mourn the desecration of, and ache to celebrate the everyday, where we mark tragedy and turn to hope, and where we give voice to the silenced and unnoticed in a busy, loud world. It is the primary vessel, I believe, for serendipity. And an apt nesting place of grace.

Going home has been poetry for me: seeing the old anew, and singing it alive.

Carolyn Weber
London, Ontario
January 2015

At the Gate of the Beautiful

Looped into ornate place,
the iron bars seem bent
on keeping us out,
imprisoning me a seeker.
I rattle all the doors
but none would budge,
not a lock would lift
with the weighted click
of absolution
from the divorce,
the break,
between what is
and
what should have been.
This contraction of
isn't
hurts.
And yet how do I know
except by the glint of this ache?
And what am I to do
with the entrustment of such pain?

At the steps of St. Peter's,
our wheels strike angle,
no ramp built in front
to detract from the glory.
My baby slumps unimpressed,
nestled in the stroller,
surprisingly quiet, this infant still,
by the shutting out, perhaps,
but more likely by the chill
of the bitter wind around us,

standing, and sitting, here, together.
Alone.

Dry leaves tornado my feet.
I notice he casts off gloves
as quickly as I replace them,
and so his little fingers have frozen
to an angry red.
I bend down, take cherub hands in mine,
rub them roughly, will them warm.
Rising, I kiss his head on the curl,
inverted question mark
peeping from beneath slipping
knit hat, the tip of a life of questions
crowning,
so that he peers at the world,
with eyes half-hooded,
wary, already,
of the dirty urban snow.
I stand tall at the helm,
uncertain where to go.

I read the bronzed plaque.
I like the history of places,
and, I must admit,
I feel if I stall,
surely some answer will crack open:
a feather will *pas de bourree*
gently through my vision,
landing at the doors as they swing
wide and wait:
but no one comes out,
and no one goes in,
so I stay and read
how the great flower
of a window came from Austria

to bloom empty blessing
high overhead.

From the shelter,
a lady named Penny
notices my son and I spinning circles
under the *No Loitering* sign.
She summons the Father.

He motions me to the back door.

My parents married here,
Long, long ago. I decide
to leave out the rest in between.
I've come to pray for them.
A doorway confession, this, I make.
Involuntarily, I step back, unsure,
afraid of offense,
of the great sin of
Inconvenience.
Come back before 4,
Father says, jingling keys in his pocket.
We close up for the night,
too many vagrants, you know.

My son arches wisely.
I apologize, turn quickly,
push stroller through park,
past the Victory statue
with burning sword held high,
for men who have died
pro patria.
I push, too, through
the prayers unsaid.

Darkling it is now, and too cold to stay.

The bells ring at my back.
My son twists toward the sound,
but not I.
I look ahead, and with steps slow
on path slick with false spring,
littered and winding,
through the park's gate
we take our solitary way.

Intention

Surely creation was not purposed
for such skittishness?
For bird to flicker from finger with wary eye;
for beaver to duck and weave, known only by
streamers of river behind?

How to account for the deep shaft of awe
through which we are hurled,
lay low and flung high –
when sunrise or sunset comes into view
or rainbow colours thundering sky?

The intake of joy comes as sharp
as a death rattle, soft trill,
the realizing thrill, exhaling
of what no one can see, and live ...

except for the poet, returning
with shaded spark: ink nekyia dark
and page gleaming like those
who roll away stones from our tombs.

Winter Reign

It amazes me that a living thing
should bear the accumulation
of hardened water,
puffed into cold and light:
that animus should be
diademed with such indifference.

It is one thing for the trees,
who stand still, embarked to sky
with outstretched boughs richly frosted,
or for the crouched bushes,
preferring needles to skin,
to prop rounded bundles
of transient white against ever green,
or ever blue, as in the case of our spruce.

It is quite another for the beating heart
and heated breath of moving mammal
to lift its head, as the deer before me,
and meet my gaze with eyes unchanging,
ears pricked straight
through a crown of snow.

Winter Solstice

Night almost touches night.
The days slivered silver between black--
they blink short--
with merely a deer's leap between them.
The moon becomes our sun,
casting long shadows through bare trees,
so that spiders' legs vein the yard
where fireflies once glinted.
In such a furnace of frost,
all gets burned down to its basics:
the world in black and white,
and me,
somewhere in between.

The Cottage in Winter

For my sister

The sky sifts snow,
like flour it falls,
lightly, so that a single breath
could blow it all away.
I sit within, flames licking heels,
waiting for words that may never come.
trusting that the lake rewards patience,
though it is frozen, now.

Summer haunts here.
A thread through my childhood
these old beams and boards,
buried in new, so that only the space
speaks of the sadness of loss
and the laughter of children
still within us, deep within us,
the one sound eternal.

There is a spirit in this space
I touched gently once.
I reach for it now,
brushing against time,
and just when nothing seems
recognizable, ours,
over the door of this white world
winks a strip of peeling green paint.

Frozen Lake

As with all things elemental,
it is difficult to tell
where one is not the other
and the two become one.
Dunes of sand, hardened with cold
so that my foot leaves no print;
waves of ice, suspended in air
so that no rush nor roar nor hint
of lap finds ear.
Here, the beach paints a still life,
chilled to its bones
of brittle driftwood and scarred shell.
As with all things elemental,
bound fast to the earth
with a force that must break what is
removed from the spell.
A solitude interspersed
with the cracking
of adjustments,
creaking and groaning from below
echo my step upon threshold.
And from somewhere, above,
across pewter sky,
the geese, flung on fog,
homeward, cry.

Oh, How We Danced

It's hard to believe this was once
a lakeside carnival town,
that a boardwalk split the beach,
crowding with tourists,
children sticky with orangeade,
the drink that made this port famous,
and bathers in rented costumes,
bloomers to the knees.
So many things to set one whirling:
a ferris wheel, a carousel,
even a roller coaster they say,
and an incline railway scaled the hill,
while another train took you down to the shore,
where waves lapped at the largest dance hall in Canada.
All was a bustle, bright and gay!
Such noise, activity, litter and glitter;
war-time-wise play,
mixed with investor exuberance.
The Coney Island of the Great Lakes!
they called it,
where we danced the night away.

But no one would know, to look at it now.
Sands stretch empty, with a lone restaurant or two.
Not a single stone, cog or wheel in view;
tracks rust, weeds cover the pier,
steps up the hill lead nowhere.
No music but the cry of gulls, drifting high,
no need to land, no open hand
flinging food extravagantly.
The planks of trails now paved silent,
and Lovers' Lane eroded away.
Only a car or three

an hour, sometimes a day,
where there had been lines bumper to bumper,
radios blaring with the heat
of sun and bodies and youth and a hunger
to ride this great adventure of progress, together.

Pull the curtains back, walk the small dog,
eyes strain in whittled face of the memory-teller,
to see again all there is to see.

Ribbons of snow blow ahead of me,
smoothing the secret folds of the sand.

Rooting

Can the sorrows ever be rooted out?
For even when pulled,
clumps of dark earth clinging,
wired with tiny tendrils of translucent flesh,
some hole remains.
An absence, it is,
that speaks of once holding
and growing dear
a place, a touch, a heart,
within mine.

The Unchangeling

Times, indeed, have not changed.
No babe switched at birth,
mortal or immortal,
matters now.
It is finished,
and we must live in the conclusion.
The stone throwers are unearthed
from bloody lot
to toss and strike and shatter
again and again.
Those who devise in their hearts injustice
and mete out violence on the earth,
those who pit one against the other
while claiming to be their brother's keeper:
voted, elected or promoted forth –
a tribunal of wealth, power and decree,
to which the innocent and poor are subject –
Ah, to such as these there are no words.

If I tell you, you will not believe me.
If I ask you, you would not answer.

No, the times, indeed, have not changed.
Nor has the unchanging outside of time.
Surely the righteous will be rewarded.
Surely there is a God who judges the earth.

DeLaurier Homestead

The cemetery startled me.
Turning the bend among the wild asparagus
I bristled like a dog
sniffing the air ripe with onions
so that my eyes teared
in time for the sight of tombstones,
the semblance of grief,
centuries too late,
I.
How weary those bodies must have been,
laid here to much desired rest,
bent low by tilling and leveling
and the relentless timing of harvest,
so that a mere tap
was all needed to complete
fall into grave.
The sinking into sodden earth
of hardened forms,
like sticks in the marsh
dropped by red-winged blackbird
diverted from nest.
Once young, lythe bodies,
sweating from work in August haze,
they.
Men sucking boots out from soggy field,
each step seeking deliverance,
a pilgrimage among unforgiving trees:
the Carolinian forest draped heavy with vines,
trapping.
Women housed in small spaces,
damp with the cooking, the cleaning, the sewing,
the countless duties and distractions
of children, animals, house,

of keeping things
alive.

Perspiration dripping, sweetly sour smelling,
wipes from foreheads with bare arms,
dabbed from cheeks with aprons,
Shirts stripped, skirts dropped,
for dipping in lake at end of day.
Angry waves warm to the west,
whipped by currents from the tip;
cold calm to the east,
sheltered by marsh slowing all
to a dead
stop.
On the porch, rock back and forth
the old, too gnarled to swim, too tired to float,
surrounded by sweet grass,
they point to the land,
where I now stand,
graven words at my feet,
and dream only of the lake,
and wait to rest.

One Incessant Fly

One incessant fly
is all it takes to distract
from the pleasant perfection
of a sunny afternoon.
One fly's dive-bomb droning,
zoning in upon my
focused concentration
is enough to shatter
every thought mid-air:
shards cutting everywhere
so that idea falls to page,
broken.
One fly who escapes my wrath,
who frustrates my swing,
eludes my rolled magazine,
my shoe, a book, anything
flung at small winged demon
with all the futile strength
of Sisyphus rolling his rock –
yes, this single black speck
owns the power to destroy
an entire realm of serenity,
to blemish an otherwise
flawless vista.
Fly, you are an itch
I cannot reach ...
a petty curse, the pursing
of lips instead of a kiss,
the dissing of my bliss,
a pinch staunching any
overflow of thanks. Oh, this
must be hell indeed:
beauty and peace all around,
mercilessly intercepted by
one incessant fly.

Mothering

"To raise bare walls out of bare earth
was the utmost they could do."
I now understand how Woolf's words fell.
There is only so much I can do,
and much less that I can do well.
I have no room of my own.
Rather, my days are patterned
by the making of meals, the sorting of socks,
the turning and unturning of beds,
the stroking of hair, the patting of heads,
teaching, encouraging, disciplining,
raising up so much more than mere walls
seem to suggest.
Little bodies entwined about my legs,
I am vined with requests,
pruned with demands,
queries and quarrels swarm me:
I kiss and fix and swaddle and wipe –
my life blurs all verb
with no punctuation
except for the dash of sleep between days –
the comma of a cuddle,
(the aside of such awe hidden in the question
of how can this love be? And the silence of
a grace beyond answers)
and yet …
here is my space
in the privilege of this race
for a crown that cannot be lost:
my exclamation mark of a soul
formed to glorify God,
with a face beaming upwards to receive Him!

Fathering

Exactly one fortnight
to the hour my father breathed his last,
the dead birch fell.
The wind rushed in my ears as I slept;
I woke to something missing,
to the slowly sudden piercing of grief:
a skeletal arm stretched across frosted grass,
fingers pointing accusingly at my house.
When I walked outside to examine
the remains early that morning,
I stood dumb to see
how its branches speared the earth,
shafts shot so deep that I could not extract them,
no matter how hard I braced my boot
and pulled with the useless traction
of gloved hand.
A friend joined me in my marveling:
Following tornadoes, she told me,
matter of factly,
I have seen stalks of straw hurled at such force
stick fast like arrows in the trunks of trees,
and twigs needlepoint the sides of houses.
The wounding of winds,
and yet the great fall taking place
not when the children were at play
as was the usual day in our yard:
but with them dreaming of trees
tall and green and waving,
safe, saved,
in their beds.

Spring at my Window

The morning is brimming with sounds springing –
the singing of birds, each note distinct;
the humming of insects, all a whiz and a whir:
growing are the buds –
before my very eyes! –
of the climbing tree outside my window
opened in surprise to a fresh new world
pulsing green into this hesitant warmth …
the thaw this year a long time coming.

What jubilee now radiates forth where
only yesterday winter's hush muted
all in grey slumber, silvered still:
bright white worn away, polished quiet,
by tenacious chill.

Oh, the thrill! The quickening –
finally, the whole of the vision –
the cycle, a circle, a glimpse
of the tapestry comes into view,
this plait. Indeed! Indeed.
They also serve who only stand and wait:
and a longing fulfilled is sweet –
ah, loving sweetness –
to the soul.

Preface to True North

I wrote this baker's dozen of poems upon my return to my hometown, London, Ontario, Canada, after much wandering around the wide, wide world. I love the trees here, the scents of the seasons, the extremes in temperature, the moodiness of the sky. When I left here, I sensed God but didn't know Him; now I *know* Him and He drenches my senses, even here, where I had been suspect but unrealizing before.

We know the earth revolves around a central core and we refer to that as being "**True North**." However, we also have the **magnetic North** which is several miles away from "True North." When it comes to successful navigation (such as for airplane pilots), you had better know the difference. It is imperative to know which "north" you are following. In Isaiah 14: 13, we see that during Sennacherib's reign (and Lucifer's fall), he refers to "...the greater recesses of the north," meaning Mount Zaphon (or the heavenly dwelling place of God). I find these "northern reflections" fascinating, for on a symbolic level it seems that people need to get their direction precise or they will miss the spiritual north of the heavens, or the *true way* of their lives.*

Fellow Canadian writer Margaret Atwood declares in her poem "Journey to the Interior" that a "compass is useless." Indeed, a man-made compass *is* useless when trying to navigate toward the kingdom within. There are journeys toward destinations marked by the stars, which cannot be measured or estimated with any kind of human precision.

True North cannot be contained by any map. Rather, through my inexpressible longing for lines that will meet in a future I cannot see, I find my way home.

* Thanks to my friend Jack Weber (no relation) for this distinction and spiritual insight regarding "true north."

Upon Returning to the Forest City

When I die then to live,
bury me under these trees
whose leaves turn
silver and green
silver and green,
whose rustling moves me,
and whose stillness –
still –
speaks to me.

For even amidst the bustle of being,
sirens and screeches and the traffic
of everyday living
their arms wave praise,
reach high to embrace
the secret of the skies
from the humility of roots
firmly in earth.

May I rise with the tree
on the dance
this dance always,
for always,
welcoming me home.

Tenure

Balanced precariously
on the tree limb outside my kitchen window
the squirrel surveyed his prospects –
the well-stocked birdfeeder
just out of his reach.
Then, with the fearless precision
of a circus performer
he tucked head to tummy
and tumbled –
a perfect somersault over the bough
with just enough force to clear
the gap

and hang

for a few suspended moments of gluttonous glory
at the feeder tray:
Victorious!

Until gravity took its toll
and forced the completion of the circle
so that he sat forlorn though fat-cheeked
back on the bough,
chewing his seeds as I did my thoughts.
Then, giving his face a dissatisfied rub,
he repeated his routine,
an acrobat lost in his funhouse,
a gymnast compelled by the ever elusive 10.
Bemused, captivated …
by such death-defying dining …
I sipped my coffee
an artful voyeur

safe
behind my shield of glass.
Over and over and over again
he completed the maneuver
tuck and roll
grab and gorge
to return and sit and rub his eyes
befuddled and dissatisfied still.
Compelled by what? I wondered.
A gene? A dare?
Or the thrill of the momentum?
Or simply, so simply,
The hunger?
I fell into the old habit
Of feeling like clapping ...

... Until I saw the cardinal below
bright as a poppy
bobbing in for a lackadaisical feast
from the feeder's overflow spotting the grass below.
He pecked at his leisure,
seemingly unaware of the
tumbling act directly above.
Upon his fill,
he left the ground in a crimson streak
for the sky of oh so June blue -
cresting my evergreen, dotting its top;
then celebrating his contentment in notes
Resounding!

And so, for the squirrel,
still madly spinning for his supper,
I emptied my cup
and held my applause.

Promotion

A strange pendulum,
>> the squirrel sat
swinging
>> stuffed into a birdfeeder
much smaller than his plump self,
>> so that only his tail
bushed out
>> like a brown boa
gaudily dressing
>> the weather-worn wood.
Tick,
>> tock
tick,
>> tock.

The moments of his meal
>> moved in motion
with the music of time.

Again, I sat bemused and transfixed,
at my kitchen table,
as I might have before a dinner show,
except that it was brazenly breakfast.
When suddenly,
the feast was indeed broken:
a sudden snap –

and the crack of what seemed so solid below.
With a thud,

the squirrel sat, stunned,
having plummeted to the ground:
his gluttonous weight too much
for the frame,
for the seeds that could never satisfy.

I laughed out loud,
happy to be home alone,
with the timing and rare silence
to bear witness
to such a comical event
in the live theatre of my backyard.

Stunned on the seed-speckled snow,
the squirrel remained motionless
for much longer than squirrels tend to do.
He cocked his head right at me,
and we locked eyes
                 in *kairos*
through glass.

He was not amused
at the dissipation of his provision,
at the fragmentation of all he took for granted
beneath the sureness of his feet.

I stopped laughing.
The broken house dangled from the tree:
the seed spilled …
buried now in the frosty dunes –
and the long, long wait for any thaw
far, far ahead.

Overcast

By day,
> God cast Himself over
> His people
> in the desert –
> in a pillar of cloud
> above the tabernacle.
> If the cloud did not lift,
> they did not set out –
> until the day it lifted.

Some days it is good to sit still.

> This gives me great hope
> when I still sit at my desk –
> fog inside and out –
> on these murky autumnal days
> drowning into my winter.

By night,
> when I wake in the shadows,
> heart beating against the abyss
> I pray to remember that this
> is when the cloud
> holds a flame.

Mara

When I stand here
it feels at first like a betrayal –
the greens thick with life
first burnished to gold,
then brittled to brown,
until only a few dry leaves hang high
like tattered sails on skeletal ships:
the bare masts of white birches
stand like sentinels around the dying fields
in a parameter of silent respect.
Only the death rattle of everything broken
underfoot, on bough, deep in the squirreled bush,
while the geese, high above, arrow stony sky.

But this, too, is love.

This death, this dying.
The giving up of the seed to the earth
so the earth may reclaim what was once
more than its own
but lost,
oh so lost,
for a little while …
till a vision opens deep,
a gleam of a future
growing into remembrance
of a past promise.

I look through the barren arch
full with the memory of foliage
so lush the spindled fingers tangle in its hair:
branches bent to almost breaking,
heavy with their own abundance,

and the air thick with birdsong –
vine and leaves and berries and the rush of wings –
all around me embroidered by ornate hand,
so that I sit,
centered,
as though a word on a medieval manuscript,
the margin around me,
illuminated.

But now I am on a different page.
Today there is no margin, no center,
no illumination.
The white sheet of advent has not yet come
and so darkling I listen
as the murky November sun
can hold its breath no longer
and drowns, drowsily, to night.

I shiver.
Bitter:
a taste
and a temperature –
of inner,
and outer,
weather.

The only thing that makes these
sour waters sweet –
that brings the germ from earth
to burst forth green,
that presses page yellowed and curled,
afresh:
first a rattle, then a shout!
The noisy holiness –
the assured jubilee –
secreted deep within the silent seed

crushed beneath my feet . . .

as I wander home
in the dark …

is the touch of God.

The Seasonal Resurrection

The seasonal resurrection has two names:
spring,
and
vernal equinox.
But I must wade
through this world
shaken like a snow-globe
so that everything swirls and drifts within,
before knowing which
captures the sighing and the singing
for me, that year:
the verb blossoming into being
and coiled noun of potential?
Or the sash of green
wrapped around the waist
of a moment,
weaving into and spinning out of
time?

The Return of the Thought-Fox

(Or, Upon Reading Ted Hughes at Midnight While Up
Late With Blank Page)

The other night
the thought-fox crept
into my backyard
while I lay sleeping.
I knew it had been there
by the prints it had left:
patterned transgressions in the moon glow,
on the otherwise
tabula rasa of snow,
excepting one corner, though,
dog-eared by a final mad scramble to escape
under my gate
as I woke.

Under the Tree

Though the world sleeps
in gaudy unremembrance
the still, small voice
becomes an infant's chance
to startle us to cry,
Out, Out, Out!
of ourselves
from the starlight
of the sky
and so deliver us
from our denials cold,
by the gift of lasting gold,
and relieve us of our bitterness
anointed now by frankincense
embalmed by this winter
in the wrap of myrrh:
This Holy Exchange
of God for man
that bedazzles kings
and leads the wise
to trust all things
which are not necessary
that I understand.

December 26th

The tree sits forlorn,
the garlands droop,
the cheer deflated.
Even the ornaments lack luster.
The mistletoe has lost its pucker
and the wreaths hang, tired.
The wrappings strewn over the floor
sign remnants of presents undone,
given and guessed:
their secrets,
gone.

The wise men, too, have left,
albeit a different route,
back to their homes,
de-gifted and mute:
struck speechless by the politics
and the glory.
The cows and sheep
now wander under a starless sky,
nuzzling pebbled earth
to appease their hunger.
Sealed tight from all soaring,
the swallow huddles
as the wind whistles through the barn,
the snow no longer picturesque –
just cold.

And so now, under this sky of slate
the growing starts:
the infant into the child,
the child into the man,
the man who will heal as his own body is pierced,

who will restore
through his own deposition.
And his mother will again
grieve with the pain
from this re-birthing into the ancient of days
far, far
after Christmas.

This birth and growth and death
common to all,
and yet in one singular case,
the divine and the human
and the Love
are the same,
so relentlessly regardless
of the date.

White Silence

It's appropriate that the colour
should match the sound –
such lack of both
or perhaps,
rather,
such an intense abundance
that there is no
colour
or sound
to hold it all
in this broken world,
the light must bend,
the colours refract
so that white gleams together
every shade,
the silence,
every sound.

White sky, white trees,
white ground,
white falling ...
frozen light in motion.
All quiet –
quieting –
in the way the tiny, perfect,
individual flakes
accumulate in great mounds
balanced on delicate boughs:
this sight alone of such improbability
seems proof enough, I think.

The whole world washed white
and the holiness of it all

so loud around me
that it can only settle into a
silence unspeakably profound:
The proclamation
to a people yet unborn –
for He has done it.

River's Edge

He had been particularly cranky
the past few days;
the betrayal of his cries harder to hide,
his discontent more difficult to soothe,
fussy, irritable
as though he could sense the impending launch –
and perhaps,
as an infant prophet
he well could –
though it would take murder
to set all in motion.

She had many to choose from, some quite ornate,
others, larger,
marked with the tradesmanship of her tribe,
any of them much more appropriate,
you might think,
for cradling one who would speak with God.

But she wanted to make the basket herself.

She chose papyrus.
Rendering unto Pharaoh's,
what was Pharaoh's –
while keeping the dearest coin for herself.
Peeling the slender rods,
circling close to the core,
she worked until her fingers bled,
fingers that shook as they braided
stalk upon stalk,
forging a silent design of silent sorrow,
a bowl that carried best
by not filling;

impenetrable by even
a single tear.

During the season of its making,
she remained bent over her work,
the fine baby restless at her breast.
With the tilt of her chin,
she could kiss the top of his head, nuzzle his hair,
whenever she wished,
and drink in the newness of his skin,
that sweet infant scent,
a fragrant balm
to her heart cracked wide.

So, in this bowed bearing,
each plait became a prayer,
the weaving became the way,
until she could no longer tell
the difference between night and day:
the river ran a murky silver
in her dreams,
rushing up to meet her
swirling all around them
with its serpentine streams.
A mother,
a daughter,
and a princess,
bathing.

At first her fear rattled the reeds,
anguish made the river bank slick:
what is this sleight of hand,
this double-edged weaving?
This eluding of one death
only to meet another?

The river at the reeds' roots moved not,
but curled like a snake,
in waiting …
and yet the stalks grown tall above her
swayed leafless in the wind,
with a rush like resounding waters
pouring over her head –
sedge topped with dense clusters
dusting the intangibility
of sky.

Breathing deep their brushing joy,
she drowned to herself
and danced with the stalks,
danced with her fingers as she wove,
plaiting her strain
to their song.
As it is for those who mother-love,
her fingers grew steadier and steadier
with the twisting repetition.

On the third day, the finished basket
sat humming in her lap.

Such an ordinary thing to the outward eye:
no indication of its beginning,
of its heritage or place.
Though fine in texture,
its handiwork lay hidden
by a coat of no real colour,
tar and pitched against all beauty,
the vessel now secured
against the seepage of the mire.

But to the inward eye:
an ark of one

built from a flood
of tears and milk and blood.

She lined the river cradle
with a single palm leaf
and then lay inside
a sacrifice no smaller than Abraham's.

And so the papery boat
floated ...
A simple, child's tabernacle
on the rippling grace of the river.

And from the muddied shallows
the danger of drowning
tips to the promise of refuge
in the gentle push
from the river's edge
of a faithful hand.

Every Desire

Every desire, every want
nicks, curves my fiery body
into a key,
cooled,
for a door without a lock.

Every thrill, every bliss
gasps, drills a keyhole through
to
Your inconceivable Glory.

Every despondency, every sorrow
blows, carries my soul
like a feather

falling ...

drifting ...

coming to rest
in Your open palm –
returned to the dove
You put to your lips.

Morning After Windstorm

Like all pilgrims,
I wanted to get to the holy place
without getting muddy.
I could see the glimmer through the brambles,
or so I thought.
The semblance or suggestion
of even a gleam
seemed gracious enough.

But the obstacle ahead took my breath away.

Across the narrow path
a birch had toppled,
victim to the windstorm the night before.
While I drank my tea by the fire,
nodded, then plodded upstairs to bed,
this tree shuddered and cracked and finally fractured
like a great white bone
scissoring the morning path,
posing a perplexing perpendicular
to my journey along the horizontal:
This pilgrimage to somewhere I knew
mere steps couldn't take me,
yet for which I had no other way to start.

As I edged by its splintered silence,
forced into the indignant slide
of the surrounding mire,
its marrow caught my coat.
Snagged, I stared into its brokenness
and traced with my old boot the cleft
its toppled mightiness
sharped into the mud.

I stepped into its suffering,
where, for a moment, I stayed, still,
studying the broken body,
until my hand reached out for its papery skin.
I peeled a strip,
pocketing with care the delicate parchment scroll.

Then, suctioning my sole
out of the hurting earth
with a sickening snap,
I pulled free from mud and marrow,
and slipped beneath the whispering
of its mourning brethren
to the holy place,
or,
at least,
toward the brambled glimmer.

Preface to Summering

I am a lover of the seasons. The sun, the snow, the smells
… I come from a land that lives out its cycles with overt
exhibition and resplendent subtlety. Bare limbs bring
forth sweet buds which explode seemingly overnight into
verdant foliage and then burn in bursts of russet flame.
The palette in this country goes white in the winter;
intimate notes from the wind are sketched in frost on the
window panes. In the day, hills pour like milk under
murky sky; at night, diamond-glint expanse stretches out
in the moonlight, soundless as the pause before re-birth.
Often the whiteness comes accompanied by a cold so
cold it burns.

But summer always wades in, fresh at first, then growing
heavy and hot. The earth rolls out green, as far as the eye
can see – a green so vibrant it jumps off the page of this
reality, and almost hurts the eyes of the soul with a
searing glory bright to behold. Air, thick with warmth
wraps around one like a mantel of softest cloth. In
sunshine everywhere, birdsong rises like praise. Cicadas
razor the languid afternoon, cricket-song blankets the
night. All is ablaze, all sounds, dimming and quieting
only before the advancing majesty of the storm – under
the weight of glory reflected in the summer sky.

I entered this earth, this place, this life, in the very midst
of summer. The sun rules my bones and blood. And
through this body, I feel my way into the body of words
and the Word. In this small collection of poems written
under the sun and the Son, I hope you will join me in the
delight of finding your way, too.

Chipmunked

Who is this visitor from Porlock?

The one who has broken the spell …
I jerk my head up at the rattle,
lose my tune on the keys.

The watering can tips over of its own accord.

Is my backyard haunted?
I wonder such –
in the brightness of day
I am as confident as the cloudless sky,
a bowl of blue overturned on me –
I am sure it is not,
that I am not.

But ask me the question
in the shadows,
in the darkling and gloom,
in the stillness of moonlight
when the clatter and clang
come from within.

The chipmunk from the toppled watering can
sits blinking,
having spilled out too
from the damp dark,
then quickens into the dazzlement
of light and garden and green
under bowled over sky.

Archery

A finch flashes golden arrow
from the bough bent like a bow
searing my line of vision
with beauty of such precision
that I cannot finish thought on page
but only dangle –
in awe –
and sage-seeking delight

suspended in the flight

from stooped blindness
to risen sight.

Burning Bush

As I round the corner
on my morning walk
the sun catches them
glinting among the leaves,
golden sparks on greenery:
a bush on fire!

I am
the catalyst.

The explosion takes place as I pass.

Clouds of golden finches burst forth:
a fireworks display
in celebration
of this holy day.

Falling Sparrows

Our hands were so unalike:
hers, frail and lined,
worn with years of loving and giving.
Mine, soft and smooth
as a freshly opened petal.
Even very young,
I would study them
as we sat
side by side
on the antique couch
and marvel at the difference,
weave my fingers into hers
until they were knotted,
grafted together,
branches from one tree
veined through generations.
I held these hands tight,
grabbed firm the gnarled roots
but they would slip from me
as she lifted her glasses to wipe away
tear upon tear
for a place I could not see,
a place from which she had been gone,
so far for so long.

Grandpa's ghost creaked the floor boards at night
in the house that had birthed and lived and deathed.
We'd huddle together and listen:
there was no fear,
only hope
that he would come for her
on the same week day we were each born.

In the afternoon

sunlight refracted off the glass sugar bowl
as big as a cookie jar
with a long spoon that could reach
all the way to the bottom.
My sister and I would shovel
large scoops of the white
into steaming brown,
stir and blow and sip
a syrupy nectar,
pretending age,
until the china pattern peeked out
from the bottom.

The old ladies who came to visit,
who spoke in a tongue even older,
would take our cups,
read the leaves,
nod and smile,
or frown and whisper.
Around us, diamonds danced
as the sun lowered through sugared glass.

Outside, the sparrows pecked
at the feast from my grandmother's hand,
the one I would hold later in mine,
as she prayed and wept and storied us into sleep.

Summer of the Butterflies

There must have been a larger crop than usual
the autumn before,
an abundance of winter cocooning –
for the emergence came as swift and thick
as the foliage on the trees.
Only a short time before,
world had laid silent, dark.
Bare branches marbled sky
all ochre and shadow
after having been washed white.
It seemed such a short, sweet season
of humming beneath the surface
before all sprung forth:
and now the full glory before me,
around me,
verdant as Eden,
the first living colour.

Who thinks of such a hue?
Who dares bring it forth,
not with meager touch
but in bold, wide strokes
so that the brilliancy hurts the eyes
as it heals the soul?
An emerald embrace,
singing and breathing and buzzing,
a-whir with life,
from the vibration of the dragon fly
crossed wing in flight
to the crack of the baseball bat,
insects living and moving and dying
in the time it takes the children
in the schoolyard nearby

to run in diamonds,
dream some dreams,
to huddle and cheer,
before the bell.

Everywhere I go this summer,
the butterflies surround me.
They pour off the breeze,
scatter from the bushes,
dust the path,
and rise from the grass
in synchronized salute
as I pass.
I have never been so lit
by being so alighted upon.
Butterflies adorn me like jewels:
one broaches my shoulder,
another crowns my hair,
a live ring for my finger,
wings beating to my pulse
when I hold out my hand.
Others flutter against my cheek,
gentle as kisses
blown from a secret admirer.

Such finery while I do the mundane!

Pull weeds, clean the yard,
walk to and from the school,
with little hands clasped tight in mine.
The children laugh in delight
at the lighting
and I am reminded of walking
with my grandmother
up the street warming with spring
swathed in butterflies and stories,

my hand, then the little one, held tight in hers,
folded together in this sort of walking prayer.
And her dimming eyes bright with memories
so much like my mother's now:
eyes that look into mine
with the shared knowledge
of babies and worries and wonders and death,
eyes that crack open my cocoon
and unfurl my wings,
eyes that see me as they once flew.

And I suddenly taste the harvest,
understand the jubilee:
the winged celebration of my coming home.

Toad Spell

The trespasser does not go
undetected
through our garden.
My daughter gasps with pointed finger
while the boys arm themselves with sticks.
The accused freezes in his tracks
gulping and billowing
guilt and apprehension.

We form a circle around him
but then withhold our stones.

I understand the fear,
the judgment
the trepidation at being beheld
as too flawed to pass.

Somehow, without words,
we all step back.
My son moves his dump truck
out of the way
opening the path to safety.
We wait with bated breath
For the leap ...

But it does not come.

The children grow impatient,
go off to other things.
Only I stay and wait and meet
his unimpressed gaze.

Soon a girl needs some juice,
a boy topples from a tree;

I administer hugs and snacks and band aids.

When I return to the prince in waiting,
he is gone.

Dark soil stares up from where
he had bellowed so silently –
no pebble disturbed, no track or trail,
no signs of the slipping away ...

Only the garden made emptier now
somehow
by the unfulfilled promise
of a kiss.

Foretaste and Tell

I imagine that in the world renewed
the air will smell this sweet:
greenery lilac and rose bejeweled,
lily of valley at my feet.
I surmise that birds will dash and sing
as they do on this clear day,
with vibrancy flung from every wing,
song-balm dropped in notes each way.
I rest assured that all our tears
by a gentle hand are swept
and that everything that pains and sears
will be from us far kept.

Is this but a hope quaint,
a vision of child's play?
And yet it takes a child or saint
to see through to the Way.
For it is moments like this we seek
when all about us is a caress
of time on eternity's cheek,
free of care and loss and duress.

In the longing and the foretaste
comes the telling of mind and heart
that our lives are not a waste
when self ends where God does start.

Sylvan Secrets

When I enter the woods
and listen
these are the secrets
it tells me:

that the diseased tree
attracts the incessant
knocking of the woodpecker;

that the butterfly's soaring
is birthed from patience –
in cocooned metamorphosis,
to the pumping of blood
from inmost body to outmost tip,
to the drying of dust on wing;

that the cardinal sings clearest
from the top of the evergreen;

that in the running of sap
and rubbing of crickets' legs
and rushing of wind
and rippling of grass

I am not alone.

Heartened

Because you were courageous
and loved me as you were first loved,
you reminded me into my heritage,
you helped retrieve what had been lost,
so that now I know
somewhere long ago
joy was chosen for me
over all other things
and that I would not choose differently
but rest in the perfect peace
of such mutual agreement,
such longing in synch
with the music of the spheres –
and so I touch the ring of eternity
enwrapping my pulse
and give thanks for the beat of your heart,
for mine.

Open Window at Night

The night lies thick and still outside my window.
Children sleep hard in twisted sheets.
Husband snores, cocked back in old chair,
left over worries spill
from his lap,
the day's work never done,
only darkened with setting sun,
and so laid dormant
until revived by chaos and coffee
in the morning rush.

I should sleep, I know,
but I am not drowsy.
How can I be?
I sense its advance …
summer moving in the dark,
growing bright under dark surface,
pushing warm and sweet through to light.

I do not have to close the window tonight:
the air no longer crisp, but tender.
Each morning now will be
warmer, brighter, come earlier …
I shiver with the reward
as I stretch from winter's hunch
and drink in cricket song.
Yes, each day will grow longer now …
one night at a time.

Summer Storm

Sleepiness heralds its arrival,
long before the actual rumbles start to sound.
My eyelids droop, weighed down by heavy air,
and everything seems to soften into slow motion.
I want to cocoon and sweetly sleep,
stretch out beside melted cat
beneath the cool hum of ceiling fan
and slumber deep.

I read somewhere that the foretelling drowsiness
is a fact-based phenomenon,
something to do with ions tumbling through the air,
charged and charging.

But I think
perhaps this need to sleep is conflict avoidance
on my part –
wanting to dodge the clash
of heat and cold,
the affronting of fronts …
wanting to delay the downpour …
to distill the danger …

Long and low, thunder builds in the distance
like a kettle drum.
I head for the porch,
pocketing glimpses of lightning like front row tickets,
and tingle in anticipation of the show.

The cat yawns and rolls over,
rejecting the window into reality
for dreams.

But for me,

now caught
in this synapse
of light and sound,
sleep can wait.

Fireflies

On the night we move in
we sit in a row
on the couch
beads on a prayer chain
faces pressed against glass,
all awe, framed.
Outside, countless points of living light
dot the darkening grass.
Screen door screeches then slams
as we race outside to join the twinkling dance.
Bare feet meet cool grass,
the heat retreating with the day.
Children in night shirts,
me, in my tattered robe;
all of us, sorely underdressed
for such festivity.

What are we doing here?

Unleashed uncare wins out,
along with weariness lifted, doubts appeased.
After a full day of unpacking,
of worries and obstacles,
of sweat and second thoughts,
only now the revelation:
Joy unlimited
in the connecting of dots …
Everywhere!
The dance of living light.

Sea Glass

A little piece of me
I find by the sea.
I little piece I take
home from the lake.
A rock of glass made
to resemble diamond or jade,
edges that were jagged
of pieces broken and ragged
by ages of water smoothed,
wave upon wave soothed.
Even the beer bottle brown
made worthy of a crown,
topazed into such sheen,
it joins the emerald green
of other bottles once taken and tossed,
used up and deemed lost
but which, burnished
by baptism long,
find a new song,
cherished now in palm or pocket,
or worn as ring or locket;
beloved, a treasure,
now far beyond measure
of the world that first smashed it,
that could never fully grasp it.
Once in the rocking hold
of the One who spins gold
from the sea of suffering I see
His reflection in you and me.

Bright to Behold

These are the days, bright to behold,
that feed us into the long cold nights;
the moments for which you would give
a lifetime
for a mere handful
to keep in your soul's pockets.

A simmering day drops to tepid night
heralding the soft rain to come
at close of eyes.
The scent of anticipation –
water soon to fall from sky
on wind rushing trees;
the surf of the woods around me
lifts all world toward setting sun,
heaven-tossed,
as trees and grass and bush wave green,
bowing low to lake shivering
with cry of loon and whip-poor-will.

An offering of exultant peace,
and the writing of it, my praise.

Evergreen

They told me the roots were gnarled,
the land,
barren.
The possibility of fruit,
impossible.

I stared hard at my reflection
when I retreated from the sentences
of such annulled annunciation.
The only time in life, perhaps,
when two negatives do make a positive.
But I had to read between the lines,
ask for the for the still small voice
to come within my hearing.

In the positive sum of negatives,
God crawled into that small space with me
to do a math I could not comprehend,
perform a reading for which I had no skill.
And there He sat –
my horizon –
when you did not show.

Here.
Yet.
Along their lines.
In their words.

But I knew you would come.

In the acceptance,
I turn to go, from antiseptic cell
trusting as I touch doorknob, turning, opening
into fields overflowing with flowers

as far as the eyes can see:
soul-startling vibrancy!
Unembittered waters rise to meet my lips
and quench my thirst,
enough to drink,
yet not to drown
by the keeping of a promise
saved by the wound of your love.

Ah yes, I knew you would come.

This king, this name for a father.

Verity, sweet verity,
the cross at the end of my doubt,
the why asked finally of truth.

All these endings
met by a beginning
that I breathed would come around again
and lift us into forever
with a new song
birthed in the summer,
together,
of our coming home.

Not Drowning but Waving

(Or, Converted Meditations on Stevie Smith's
"Not Waving but Drowning")

Someone heard me, near death,
walking on water, saving:
you were much closer than I thought
and not drowning but waving.

Dear one, this is no joke
the divide, alive or dead
heart within beats soul steps: I know the way,
You said.

Oh, yes yes yes, it would be perfect, always
(each life raised worth saving)
you were so close as to be my life
and not drowning but waving.

Bower Stroll

*Then the man and his wife heard the sound of the Lord God
as He was walking in the garden in the cool of the day, and
they hid from the Lord God among the trees of the garden
(Gen 3:8).*

Hell must be like heaven, but with a glitch:
Vista ruined by a sty in one's eye,
Delicate breeze laced with stench of rotting corpse,
Peace disturbed by a single incessantly buzzing fly,
Wrong attire worn for the temperature,
All around, the most glorious garden
tinged with poison ivy,
Vined with longing, fruitless of appreciation;
Everywhere, perfection – without satisfaction.

For those who walk in righteousness
a bower stroll
brings pleasant cool
at the close of heated day.

But for those who know their nakedness –
and blame others for their state –
we cannot stay in the sun without getting burnt
and find no relief in the shade.

About the Author

Carolyn Weber (M.Phil, D.Phil Oxford) is a bestselling author, speaker and professor. She writes from her home base in London, Ontario Canada where she lives with her husband and 4 children. Find her online at PressingSave.com

Her recent memoir *Surprised by Oxford* became a finalist for the 2012 ECPA Christian Book Award, received the Logos Book Award for the 2012 best book in Christian Living, and was awarded the Grace Irwin Literary Prize for the Christian book of the year by a Canadian Author.

Other Books by Carolyn Weber

Surprised by Oxford: A Memoir

Holy is the Day: Living in the Gift of the Present

Made in the USA
Middletown, DE
14 November 2018